MEDICINE

AUTHOR: PHIL GATES ⚗ CONSULTANT: GHISLAINE LAWRENCE

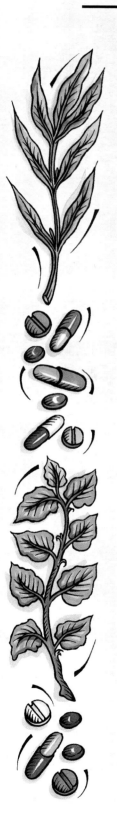

DEAR READER,

FOR CENTURIES *THE HISTORY NEWS* HAS KEPT ITS FINGER ON THE PULSE OF CHANGE. OUR REPORTERS HAVE TIRELESSLY COVERED EVERY NEW DISCOVERY AND INVENTION.

BUT IT'S THE BREAKTHROUGHS IN MEDICINE THAT REALLY CAPTURE THE PUBLIC'S IMAGINATION. NOT ONLY BECAUSE THEY AFFECT THE QUALITY OF ALL OUR LIVES, BUT ALSO BECAUSE THEY ARE FANTASTIC STORIES OF STRUGGLE AND TRIUMPH.

RECENTLY, WE BLEW THE DUST OFF OLD COPIES OF *THE HISTORY NEWS* AND PUT TOGETHER A SPECIAL EDITION TO CELEBRATE THIS AMAZING SUBJECT. SO HERE IT IS — THE STORY OF HUMANKIND'S ENDLESS BATTLE AGAINST DISEASE.

THE EDITOR IN CHIEF

Phil Gates

A NOTE FROM OUR PUBLISHER

Of course, as we all know, newspapers didn't exist as long as 10,000 years ago. But if they had, we're sure that *The History News* would have been the one everybody was reading! We hope you enjoy reading it, too.

Gareth Stevens Publishing
A WORLD ALMANAC EDUCATION GROUP COMPANY

CONTENTS

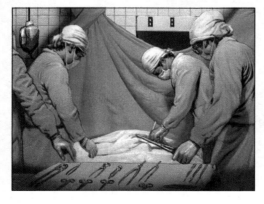

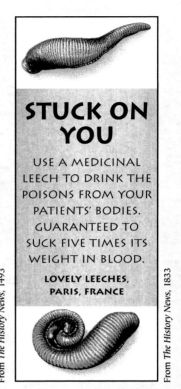
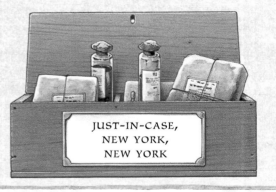
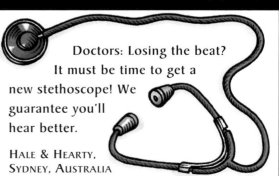
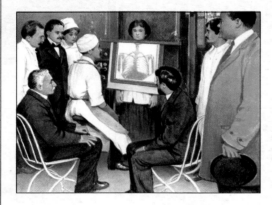

HOLD STILL! A prehistoric medicine man carefully scrapes a hole through his patient's skull.

THE HOLE TRUTH?

Illustrated by ANGUS McBRIDE

WHY ON EARTH did people back in 8000 B.C. have holes cut into their skulls? *The History News* **reports on the gruesome evidence that casts light on these dramatic early operations.**

WHEN prehistoric skulls were found with small round holes cut in them, experts thought at first that the victims had died from horrific battle wounds. But the truth has proved to be far stranger than this.

The holes are too neat to have been caused by a weapon — each one must have been carefully cut while the victim was still alive! We know this because, incredibly, some of the sufferers had lived long enough for new bone to grow around the edges of the hole.

Today, skilled brain surgeons sometimes cut into patients' skulls. This operation is known as trepanning, and it's done when surgeons need to reach the brain tissue beneath the skull. But what could have made ancient people undertake such an agonizing and delicate operation?

THE ENEMY WITHIN

Even we here at *The History News* don't know the answer for sure. Experts now believe that people long ago thought bad illnesses were caused by demons trapped in the body and that making a hole in the head would let the evil spirits escape.

To create the hole, a skilled medicine man would have used a knife with a razor-sharp flint blade to cut through the scalp and uncover bone. Then would have come the long, slow task of scraping away the bone, little by little. Imagine the terror that the helpless patient must have felt as the small hole, just over an inch across, was painstakingly created.

The last few cuts must have been the worst. One slip and either the chips of loosened bone or the knife itself would have caused terrible damage to the exposed brain.

Even today this is a difficult and dangerous operation. Yet long ago, medicine men attempted it using only crude flint tools — their achievement was truly remarkable! ✠

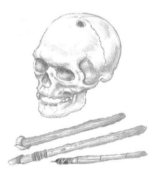

SORE POINTS: Flint-bladed knives and a patient's skull.

As time went on, some healers stopped blaming demons and spirits for every disease and searched for other explanations. They began to think that illnesses might have natural causes and looked for more effective ways of dealing with them. Over thousands of years, a great many theories about the human body were developed, and with them came a wide variety of treatments.

STICKING TO THE POINT

IN 2500 B.C., RUMORS began reaching *The History News* of a dramatic new form of treatment — Chinese healers were sticking needles into people in order to cure them! A reporter was sent to China to interview a healer and discover the truth behind these remarkable stories.

I CAN BEST explain our methods by putting them into action. Take a look at this boy here. He has a very bad cough, which I will cure by inserting these thin bronze needles into his wrists.

GET INTO THE FLOW

Don't look so horrified, it's not as painful as it looks. The needles are carefully placed so the boy doesn't feel them.

We call this treatment acupuncture, and it is based on our belief that good health depends on life-giving energy, which flows through the body along 12 major lines or pathways.

This energy consists of two opposite forces called yin and yang. And

as long as these forces are balanced, you'll stay healthy. But if either one becomes too strong, you will soon fall ill.

Placing needles into special points along the lines of energy lets out some of the extra yin or yang and brings the two forces back into balance.

You may wonder why I've put needles into the boy's wrists when it's his cough I'm treating. Well, that's because these are the points that affect the energy lines to his lungs.

Believe it or not, there are about 600 of these acupuncture points all over the body! And every single one has its own role to play in healing

different body parts. They can be used to treat every possible illness, but it takes us healers many years of study to master this difficult art.

BALANCING ACT

Of course, acupuncture isn't the only type of treatment we use. There are herbal medicines as well. I know of thousands of remedies made from plants such as ginseng, garlic, and licorice.

In China, we healers are continually looking for ways to improve our skills at treating the sick. But whether we use herbs or needles, our aim is always the same — to bring the forces of yin and yang back into balance and to bring the body back to health. ✚

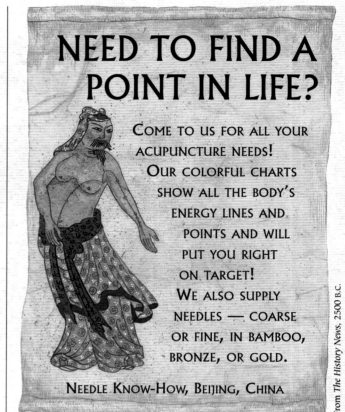

A NEW NOSE JOB!

Illustrated by SHARIF TARABAY

REPAIRING DAMAGED faces by surgery may seem like a very modern technique, but it was first performed by the great Indian doctor Susruta back in 600 B.C. A reporter for *The History News* saw him in action.

WHEN INDIA'S greatest surgeon says he's going to give a man a new nose, it's worth getting up early to watch him. The sun was just rising as I joined the students in Susruta's room here at the University of Benares in eastern India.

Susruta has taught medicine for years. He is a skilled doctor and can prepare herbal remedies, including cures for snake and rat bites, from 760 types of plants. But it's his surgical mastery that has made him famous.

CUTTING EDGE: The red line shows where Susruta cut the flap of skin.

Fresh mustard seeds had been thrown on the fire in Susruta's room. Their cleansing fumes filled the air, soothing the patient's nerves.

THE FACE OF HORROR

The poor man looked dreadful. Half of his nose had been cut off in a fight, leaving a hideous misshapen stump.

Susruta had given him strong wine to kill the pain of the operation, and now the man was lying calmly on the rug.

I watched intently as Susruta set to work. First he took a triangular leaf and set it against the center of the patient's forehead. Then he cut around it, slicing away a leaf-shaped flap of skin.

"Notice how I keep the flap attached here between the eyes," said Susruta. "That way, the

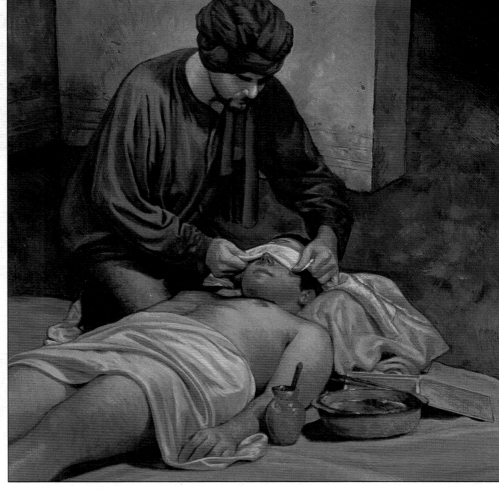

HEALING HANDS: Susruta covers the patient's new nose with a protective bandage.

skin stays alive while it heals in its new place."

He twisted the flap and folded it down over the stump. Susruta had already made some cuts on the stump, and now he pressed the edges of the new skin into these cuts so that it would stick there and heal over.

Susruta then pushed small reed tubes into both nostril spaces to give the nose a better shape. Finally, he covered it with a cloth stiffened with oil.

"This dressing will come off in four days," said the smiling surgeon, "and I'll clean the wound with boiled butter. When

the scars have healed, his nose will look almost as good as new!"

It was as simple as that! Using little more than his bare hands and his patient's own skin, Susruta had repaired the ruined face. Who but this great surgeon could have accomplished such a feat? I was honored to have seen him in action. ⊞

A PERFECT DOCTOR?

Illustrated by DARREN PATTENDEN

THE GREAT GREEK healer Hippocrates has been famous for well over 2,000 years. But back in 400 B.C., Hippocrates' medical ideas were startlingly new, as this interview with him reveals.

? Many people think diseases are caused by the gods. Is this your view?

No! That's absolutely ridiculous! A disease in the body is no more supernatural than the wind whistling down the street. People fear illness because they don't understand it. Yet every disease has its own natural, physical cause, which a good doctor can discover.

? Can you give us a few examples?

Well, the body's health is affected by many different factors.

Diet is vital. People often eat too much, or too little, or not enough of the right foods, and this upsets the delicate balance of the body.

Where you live has a part to play, too. I can predict what diseases I'll find in a village just by looking at the area around it. In marshy places, for example, I'm bound to find many cases of malaria.

? How do you know what the problem is?

The key to success is observation. A doctor must pay the closest possible attention to every symptom of his patient's illness.

I take notice of everything, down to the color and taste of the patient's urine! Then I compare my observations with what I've learned in the past to decide how serious the disease is and what action I should take.

? What treatments do you recommend?

I often advise patients to eat different kinds of food. Exercise is also very important, and so is sleep. The cure for many illnesses can be surprisingly simple, but

HIPPOCRATES:
The patient's friend.

it takes a skilled doctor to discover it.

? Do doctors need a lot of training?

Yes, but training alone is not enough. Doctors must always treat their patients honestly, telling them the truth even if the disease is severe. When sick people trust their doctors, it often gives them the strength they need to recover. ✚

ROME'S

BACK IN A.D. 200, the largest city in the world was also setting new records as the cleanest! *The History News* sent one of its reporters to Rome to find out why.

I'VE TRAVELED to quite a few cities in my time. Some were overrun with rats, most stank, and in every single one, human sewage and garbage lay rotting in the street.

So you can imagine my dread when I was sent to visit Rome, the largest city in the world. More than one million people live there, all crowded together.

But I'll say this for the Romans, they certainly know a thing or two about keeping clean.

WATER GIANTS

As I approached Rome from the east, the first thing I saw was a huge, arched aqueduct, which towered many feet into the sky.

This vast structure is one of 14 aqueducts, which together contain more than 300 miles (500 kilometers) of stone channels. Fresh water is carried by these channels from the hills around the city into Rome.

There, the water first runs into huge reservoirs and then feeds into the troughs and fountains found on almost every street. No one in the city has to walk far to collect a jug of clean water.

But the Romans don't just drink clean water,

From The History News, A.D. 200

CLEAN LIVING!

Illustrated by CHRIS MOLAN

they also use it in many other ways. For starters, most Romans bathe every single day!

Rome has more than 1,000 public baths to pick from, where people come to splash around in pools of cold, warm, and hot water.

Not only that, because they've discovered that human waste can cause disease, the Romans have built toilets for everyone to use. These toilets drain into vast underground sewers, which are flooded with water whenever it rains. The waste is then washed into the Tiber River and on out to sea.

Rome certainly is an exceptional place to live. No other city I have ever visited has taken such pains to keep its people healthy. Long live the Romans, I say — and thanks to their sewers, aqueducts, and toilets, they probably will! ✚

WELL OF LIFE: Women collect fresh water from one of Rome's many public fountains.

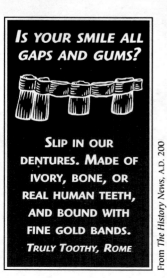
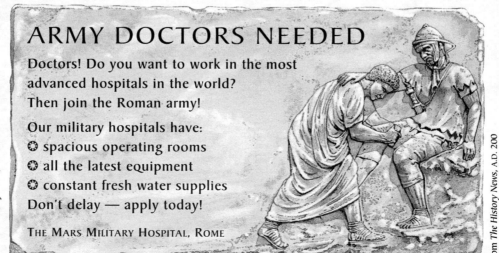
GALEN FACTS

Rome's most famous doctor was Claudius Galen. For more than 1,400 years, Europe closely followed his teachings. But what made him so special?

❖ **Born about A.D. 129,** Galen became famous for his ideas on how the body worked. It was forbidden to cut up human bodies in those days, so Galen studied the bodies of animals, such as pigs and monkeys. He assumed that all animals, from pigs to humans, were exactly the same inside.

DIG IN: An array of Roman medical tools.

❖ **Before he died in A.D. 200,** Galen wrote a number of books on medicine. He included ideas from India, as well as the teachings of Hippocrates and evidence taken from his own experiments. Galen's books became accepted as bibles of medicine and were studied everywhere.

CURIOUS CURES

Illustrated by BEE WILLEY

FOR HUNDREDS OF years, superstition played a large part in European medicine. In A.D. 1100, a British doctor sent us his book of remedies, called *Saxon Leechdoms*, which he claimed held reliable cures.

⊠ If by chance thou shouldst drink a wriggly insect in the water:
Go immediately and find thyself a sheep. Cut into it and drink the blood while 'tis still hot. If thou taketh good long gulps, all will soon be well.

⊠ If thou art being sorely tempted by the devil's tricks:
Thou needeth a powerful ointment made of many herbs. First have nine Masses said over it. Then set it under the altar of a church for a long while.

Apply this holy salve sparingly to thy body whensoever thou feelest a devil or wicked man is tempting you to harm.

⊠ For an ache that is found in the teeth:
Take between thy jaws whole corns of pepper and chew on them. It will soon be well with thee.

⊠ For swollen eyes:
Take a live crab, put out its eyes, and return it still living into the water. Put the eyes onto thy neck. All will be well.

⊠ If thou must set out on a long and weary journey:
Pull up some wormwood plant, saying, "I will take thee, lest I be weary on the way." Make with it the sign of the cross and put it in thy shoe.

OF COURSE, TODAY WE KNOW THAT THESE SORTS OF CURES WERE MORE THAN USELESS. WE RECOMMEND OUR READERS NEVER TRY THEM!

⊠ If thou art bitten by a snake:
Thou must place on the bite a salve of earwax, and hurry to ask the priest to say a prayer for thee. All will be well.

⊠ For wheezing and shortness of breath:
Take forth the fresh liver and lungs from a fox and chop them finely. Add to wine, and then drink this mixture regularly from a church bell. Very soon this cure will make all well with thee. ⊞

From *The History News*, 1150

THE DEAD OF NIGHT: During the hours of darkness, the bodies of those killed by the Black Death are carted away to unmarked graves.

PLAGUE SWEEPS EUROPE

Illustrated by GINO D'ACHILLE

EVEN TODAY THE word "plague" strikes horror into our hearts. So just picture the terror caused by the Black Death — the worst plague of all time. In 1348, our Paris reporter sent us this chilling account of the disease, just three days before he died.

LORD KNOWS, death and disease are nothing new. In our crowded cities, infections always spread quickly. But now the Black Death is turning every land into a graveyard!

It began in Asia in the 1330s, killing one person in every three. Then it swept westward. By the time it neared Europe, more than 50 million people had already died. We prayed it would stop before reaching us.

But last year, an Asian army attacked an Italian trading post in Russia and catapulted plague-infested corpses into the town. When the infected traders returned to Italy, the Black Death seized Europe in its grip.

Now it has reached Paris, and thousands are dying every day. At night, men bring burial carts to the houses of the dead. Then the bodies are taken to mass graves.

No one knows how the Black Death spreads, though doctors think it may be carried by bad smells. Many of us press sweet-smelling herbs to our noses, but it doesn't seem to save us.

My brother was one of the first to fall ill. It began with a fever. Then great boils swelled up in his armpits and groin.

The doctor told us to place dried toads on the boils to draw the poison out. But it didn't work. Blood and pus burst from the boils and black marks spread over his skin. He clung on to life for three more days, before death brought him relief.

GOD HELP US

Now I, too, grow sick. No one can save me. Some say this plague is God's punishment for the sins of His people. May the Lord have mercy! ✚

> **EDITOR'S NOTE:**
> We now know that the Black Death was caused by one of the many kinds of tiny organisms we call bacteria. This germ was carried by rat fleas and was passed to people when fleas bit them. Rats thrived in the dirty cities of the 1300s, so plague spread very quickly.
>
> Scientists finally figured out which bacteria caused the disease, and thus how to treat it, in 1894.

THE INSIDE STORY

Illustrated by SHARIF TARABAY

SURELY DOCTORS should spend their time helping the living. Yet in 1540, a Belgian physician named Andreas Vesalius seemed more interested in the dead! *The History News* **heard him explain why.**

A DEAD MAN lay on a table, covered by a cloth. Around him, a group of doctors argued loudly, all eager to be heard. All, that is, except one — the surgeon Vesalius waited patiently for silence.

The doctors had come to the University of Padua in northern Italy to hear Vesalius give a lecture. Although just 25 years old, he was turning the world of medicine on its head with his new ideas.

At last Vesalius rapped on the table for silence. "Gentlemen," he began, "as you know, I've been examining the structure, or rather the anatomy, of the human body.

SECRETS OF THE DEAD

Today I will demonstrate the crucial importance of looking at the human body for ourselves."

At this, Vesalius pulled back the cloth to reveal the corpse's abdomen.

"We don't need such a disgusting spectacle," interrupted an indignant doctor. "Galen and other ancient writers have told us all we need to know about our bodies!"

Vesalius shook his head. "The problem is," he said, "that Galen was rarely allowed to cut up actual human corpses.

He had to use animals, such as pigs, instead. But these days we can cut up the corpses of criminals. And a dead criminal is much more useful to us than a dead pig, as you will shortly see."

Vesalius sliced open the abdomen and pulled out long twisted coils of the criminal's intestines. "Here's one example," he said, as he used both hands to lift out the corpse's slippery liver. "Galen tells us that the human liver has five sections. It's true that a pig's liver does. But look! This man's liver is not divided into sections like that at all! Galen was quite simply wrong."

There was no denying it. In one stroke, Vesalius crushed a belief that was more than 1,400 years old!

There was a stunned silence. No one could doubt that Vesalius was right. Although cutting up dead bodies is a shocking idea, it's likely to transform our knowledge of the human body — and the ways in which we care for it! ✠

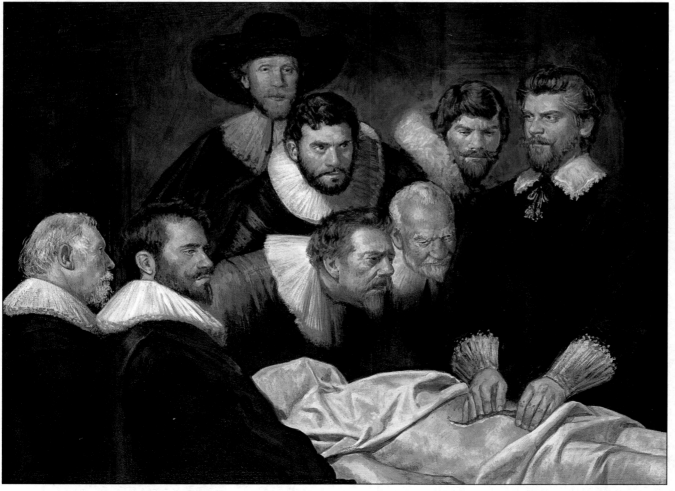

BODY OF KNOWLEDGE: Doctors eagerly peer closer as Vesalius begins his investigation of a corpse.

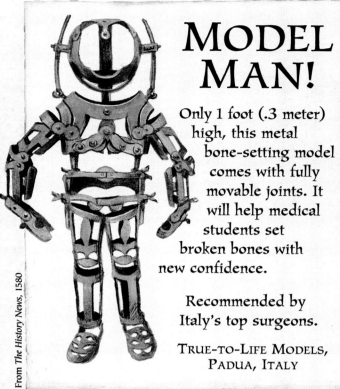
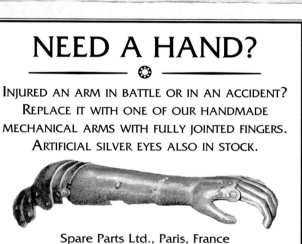
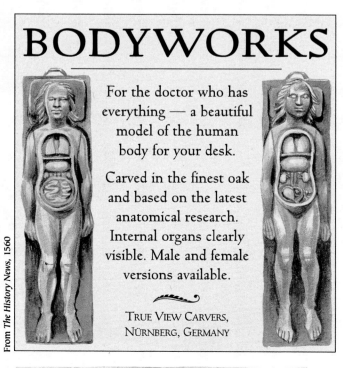

SOLDIERS' HERO: As a battle rages, Ambroise Paré tends to a wounded soldier.

KINDER CARE FOR WAR VICTIMS

Illustrated by MAXINE HAMIL

SOLDIERS INJURED in battle once suffered treatments as horrific as their wounds. In 1545, French surgeon Ambroise Paré told *The History News* how his new book would change this forever.

YOU HAVE TO be tough to be an army surgeon, or the sight of so many dying men will drive you insane.

But it doesn't mean you have to be hard-hearted. After I joined the army in 1537, I soon became sickened by the level of suffering caused by the techniques we doctors were using.

We had been taught that gunshot wounds were poisonous and that the way to treat them was to pour boiling oil over them. So that's what we did — and the men were in agony.

There had to be a better way. And one day, with God's help, I found it. I'd run out of boiling oil, so I decided to clean some wounds with a lotion made of egg yolks and rose oil.

This treatment not only caused my patients less pain but, to my joy, their wounds healed far more quickly.

My success led me to try other new methods. After cutting off a leg or an arm, it was customary to use a red-hot iron to seal the wound and stop the bleeding. I decided to sew up the cut blood vessels instead. Again, this lessened the pain and resulted in a more rapid rate of recovery.

SETTING A GOOD EXAMPLE

I have found these new treatments to be so successful that I believe it's my duty to persuade other surgeons to use them. If my book can achieve this, I will die a happy man! ✚

HEART IS A PUMP!

Illustrated by CHRIS RIDDELL

IN 1628, A LONDON doctor named William Harvey astounded the medical world when he published his revolutionary ideas about the human heart and blood system. As always, *The History News* was the first to tell the story.

It's no good appealing to my heart — it's only a pump!

From *The History News*, 1628

PREPARE FOR a shock that will set your pulse racing. The heart is just a pump! It's only a simple machine, like the pump that raises water from a village well.

So says Harvey, one of England's most respected doctors and physician to King James, in his new book on blood circulation.

Most of us notice our heart only when we're scared or in love, and it suddenly starts to pound.

So it's not surprising that we see it as the source of all of our most deeply felt emotions.

And if you asked your doctor to tell you what the heart does, he would undoubtedly repeat the old explanation given by Galen, the famous doctor of ancient Roman times.

Galen claimed that the heart was there to make blood. And what's more, the heart produced an endless supply of blood, which was delivered to other parts of the body where it was constantly used up.

But now Harvey says that Galen was wrong.

After measuring the amount of blood a heart can hold, as well as the average speed of a heartbeat, Harvey has figured out that at least a gallon (4 l) of blood flows through the heart every hour.

And, says Harvey, if the heart was producing this amount of blood all the time, our body could not possibly absorb it all. We would simply swell up, like huge blood-filled balloons.

As we know, this does not happen. And Harvey has discovered why. "The heart does not make blood," he says. "Instead, the same blood circulates endlessly around the body. It goes around and around without being absorbed, and the heart is simply the pump that sends it on its way.

You can see this whenever a blood vessel is cut. The blood comes out in spurts, every time the heart beats — just like water being pumped from a well. It's no more complicated than that!"

HEARTY LIVING

In spite of this revelation, however, Harvey is quick to point out that the heart is no less important than it ever was. We certainly couldn't live without it!

But nevertheless, it'll be impossible to think of this noble organ in quite the same way again. ✚

WHICH DOCTOR?

Illustrated by CAROLINE CHURCH

BY THE 1600s, a doctor could be a highly trained expert — or an uneducated quack. No wonder our readers were confused! In 1650 we printed our famous "Which Doctor?" advice guide.

PHYSICIAN

The most highly trained doctors are physicians, who may study for up to 10 years at a university. When they qualify at last, they're the only doctors allowed both to prescribe medicine and perform operations.

Physician

They certainly give the best treatment money can buy, but one visit to a physician will cost as much as a month's pay for most laborers, so only the very rich can afford to go to them.

APOTHECARY

These shopkeepers sell foods such as sugar and flour, as well as herbs and spices. But they will also give you advice on how best to treat your ailment, and they're skilled at mixing herbal cures.

They do not learn their trade at a university but instead spend a few years as an apprentice to a master apothecary.

Apothecaries are a great deal cheaper than physicians, and you'll find several in any town or city — a good option if you're feeling unwell.

SURGEON

Surgeons are sometimes called "bone cutters," and with good reason — they specialize in chopping off limbs. But don't ask for medicine, as the surgeons'

Surgeon

guild forbids its sale.

Make certain your surgeon belongs to a recognized guild. He'll charge you more, but at least you'll know he served as an apprentice and is qualified.

Apothecary

BARBER

Barbers don't just cut hair and give shaves! They can also deal with minor surgery, such as cutting off warts or opening up boils. They charge a small fee for their services.

Barbers have to train as apprentices and then join a barbers' guild. But before you visit one, ask about his past patients — if most of them survived, there's a fair chance you will too.

MIDWIFE

Midwives are found in every village. Most people try their local midwife first if they need medical help, so these women are very experienced. They are particularly skilled at helping out during childbirth but can easily turn their hand to any problem. They're a good source of herbal cures.

Midwives don't have any medical training and will often give their services for free.

Midwife

THE REST

They can be hard to find, but wizards and witches claim they can cure almost anything. Here at *The History News* we haven't yet dared try their services, but we know people who'd use them if all else fails! +

DEATH TO SMALLPOX

Illustrated by GINO D'ACHILLE

UP TO SCRATCH: Jenner infects a young boy with cowpox — but will it protect him from the deadly smallpox?

THE DEADLY disease smallpox raged throughout the world for thousands of years, killing millions. In 1801, we spoke to the man who finally conquered it — British doctor Edward Jenner.

❓ Why did you decide to study smallpox?

As a student in a hospital in London, I saw lots of people die from this disease. Sometimes up to 3,000 people died each year in London alone.

Smallpox is such an infectious illness, passing so quickly from person to person, that in crowded cities it spreads like wildfire. It must be one of the most widespread and deadly diseases there is.

And yet we doctors were helpless against it.

❓ But there was one way to protect people from it, wasn't there?

Oh, yes. It was called variolation, a technique that had been brought into Britain in the early 1700s by an English woman — Lady Montagu. She had watched the treatment being applied, while living in Turkey.

By giving children a mild dose of smallpox, it was hoped they would recover and never catch the disease again.

But variolation was risky. Some patients would fall ill and die.

Some would infect others and cause a new outbreak of smallpox, which would kill hundreds or even thousands of people.

❓ What gave you the idea for a possible solution?

Well, after I finished medical school, I went home to Gloucestershire to become the doctor of my local village.

I began to notice that milkmaids often caught a disease from cows, called cowpox, which gave them a mild fever and caused blisters on their hands. Yet these same milkmaids never caught smallpox, even after they had been in contact with someone who did have it.

So I wondered what would happen if you deliberately gave people cowpox. Would it protect them from smallpox?

❓ How did you go about finding out?

John Hunter, my teacher in London, always used to say, "Why just think? Why not experiment?"

This was good advice!

In 1796, I decided to try out my ideas on someone, and I chose a local boy named James Phipps. I scratched his arm and put in some cowpox pus. This gave James cowpox, but he soon recovered.

Then came the big test. Quite deliberately, I infected James with smallpox pus.

That was a nerve-racking time, I can tell you! If I was wrong, and the cowpox didn't protect him, he would almost certainly die.

But, thank God, he never showed a single sign of smallpox. The cowpox had protected him from the infection.

? How did you feel?

I was incredibly excited! More tests were needed, but I believed I was on the verge of a safe way of protecting people from smallpox.

My next tests went equally well, so I wrote a report of my findings and published it.

? And were other doctors excited?

Yes! My technique — which is now known as vaccination — is in use everywhere! Nearly 100,000 people have now been vaccinated in Britain alone. And in 1799, American doctors started vaccinating, too.

Incredible as it may sound, I believe that if we could vaccinate all the people in the world, we could destroy this disease forever! ✚

EASTERN SECRET

LONG BEFORE JENNER performed his first vaccination, people in the Middle East tackled smallpox in another way. In 1717, *The History News* received this letter from the English woman who brought the technique to Britain.

DEAR EDITOR,

I am going to tell you something that I am sure will make your readers envy the people of Turkey.

Groups of wise women make it their business to visit every village each September with nutshells full of the pus from smallpox sores. They scratch each child's arm with a needle and put in as much of the smallpox venom as can lie upon the needle's point. The children develop a fever for two days, but then recover and never catch smallpox again.

I am so impressed by this that I intend to try the experiment on my own dear son. It is risky, but surely it is the wisest course.

Lady Mary Wortley Montagu
Turkey, April 1, 1717

AN OLD ENEMY

✦ There was smallpox in Egypt during the 1100s B.C. The face of the mummified body of Pharaoh Ramses V has smallpox scars.

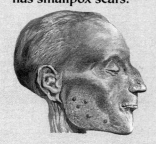

RAMSES: A marked man.

✦ The disease was first written about by doctors in China. Ko Hung, who lived from A.D. 265–313, described in detail an outbreak of the disease during his lifetime. By A.D. 1000, doctors in China were trying to prevent the disease by blowing a powder of smallpox pus up the patient's nose.

✦ Smallpox probably existed in Europe in a mild form as early as A.D. 580, but it didn't become a major killer there until the 1400s, when a more deadly form appeared.

✦ The Spanish took the disease to South America in about 1518, where it killed half the population of Mexico in a single epidemic.

✦ In the late 1960s, smallpox still infected over 10 million people worldwide each year.

NO NEEDLES: The WHO gun forces the vaccine through the skin.

✦ Finally, in 1979, the World Health Organization (WHO) ran a campaign that wiped out the disease.

MORTON KILLS PAIN

Illustrated by CHRISTIAN HOOK

THROUGHOUT history, surgery had been an agonizing ordeal. Then, in 1846, William Morton took the pain away forever. *The History News* was there when he revealed his amazing secret.

"WHERE IS MORTON?" chanted the large restless crowd of doctors and students crammed into the tiny operating room.

They had come to Massachusetts General Hospital, in Boston, to see if William Morton, a local dentist, could prove his ridiculous claim to be able to make surgery painless. Morton said he could send patients into a deep sleep by making them breathe the vapor of a strange chemical called ether.

But already Morton was fifteen minutes late. Was it all a hoax?

The patient, Gilbert Abbott, looked pale and frightened. He was about to have a large lump removed from his neck.

Finally, the surgeon, Dr. John Warren, took a last glance at his watch. Then he marched over to the instrument table and picked up a gleaming operating knife. As he did so, his helpers moved toward Abbott to strap him tightly into his chair.

THE MOMENT OF TRUTH

But at that instant, the doors flew open, and in burst William Morton, breathless and carrying a large glass globe.

"Your patient is ready," Dr. Warren said, as the panting Morton tried to regain his composure.

Morton strode across

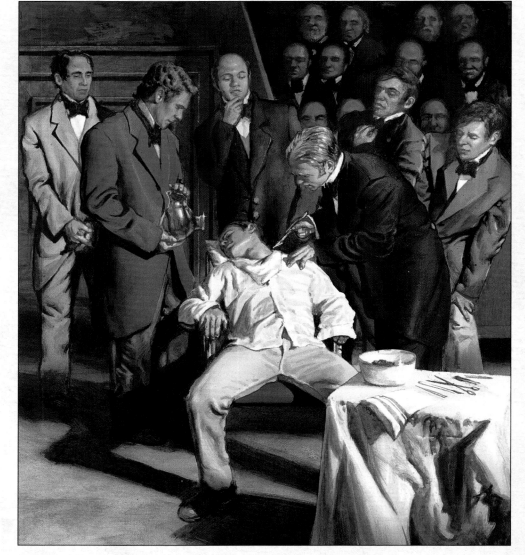

SWEETEST SLEEP: Gilbert Abbott is blissfully unaware of his gruesome operation.

to the patient and asked if he was frightened.

"No," replied Abbott faintly. "I am ready to do exactly what you tell me."

And with that, Abbott quietly followed Morton's instructions and began to breathe ether vapor through the mouthpiece of the glass globe. In moments, the patient fell into a deep sleep.

"*Your* patient is ready, Dr. Warren," stated Morton calmly, taking no notice of the surgeon's stern look.

The audience held its breath as Dr. Warren prepared to cut. No one expected that Morton's invention could possibly work. Many gave one another knowing looks, as if to say, "Just wait for the screams to begin!"

But the screams never came. The surgeon cut open the skin, severing sensitive nerves. By now Abbott should have been yelling out in unbearable pain, while the doctor's burly helpers fought to hold him still.

BEFORE ANESTHETICS

DON'T WORRY, THIS WON'T HURT!

Cartoon by TONY KENYON

But instead the room was so silent you could have heard a pin drop. Abbott never stirred.

Was the ether really protecting the sleeping patient from pain? Only Abbott could know the answer to that!

The audience waited with bated breath, as Dr. Warren completed the operation and sewed up the patient's wound. Slowly, Abbott began to wake from his sleep.

"Did you feel any pain?" asked William Morton anxiously.

TRIUMPH!

"No," replied Abbott, "I felt nothing at all."

Dr. Warren turned to the throng. "Gentlemen," he said simply, "this is no humbug!"

At these words, the jubilant crowd burst into cheers. They had come expecting Morton to fail. But instead, he'd silenced his critics — by silencing the screams of his patient.

Morton's success is bound to make news around the world. With luck, doctors will soon be using chemicals like ether in every kind of operation.

But what should we call this new invention that banishes pain?

The History News has this suggestion. Let's name it after the Greek word *anesthesia* — which means "loss of feeling." We should call Morton's vapor an *anesthetic*!

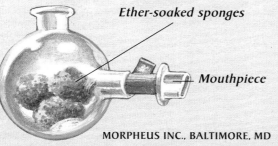
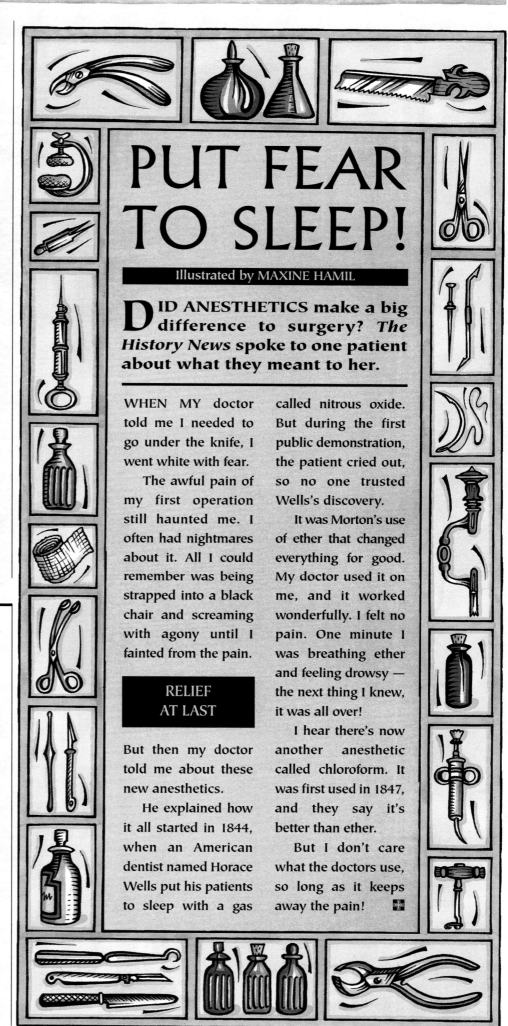

PUT FEAR TO SLEEP!

Illustrated by MAXINE HAMIL

DID ANESTHETICS make a big difference to surgery? *The History News* spoke to one patient about what they meant to her.

WHEN MY doctor told me I needed to go under the knife, I went white with fear.

The awful pain of my first operation still haunted me. I often had nightmares about it. All I could remember was being strapped into a black chair and screaming with agony until I fainted from the pain.

RELIEF AT LAST

But then my doctor told me about these new anesthetics.

He explained how it all started in 1844, when an American dentist named Horace Wells put his patients to sleep with a gas called nitrous oxide. But during the first public demonstration, the patient cried out, so no one trusted Wells's discovery.

It was Morton's use of ether that changed everything for good. My doctor used it on me, and it worked wonderfully. I felt no pain. One minute I was breathing ether and feeling drowsy — the next thing I knew, it was all over!

I hear there's now another anesthetic called chloroform. It was first used in 1847, and they say it's better than ether.

But I don't care what the doctors use, so long as it keeps away the pain!

CLEAN THIS

Illustrated by ANGUS McBRIDE

FLORENCE: THE FACTS

Florence Nightingale was born to a wealthy family in 1820. But she did not want to lead an idle, pointless life. Instead, she decided to work with the sick, although at that time, many hospitals were sordid, rowdy places.

In 1851, after a lot of arguments, her father allowed her to train in a hospital in Germany.

In 1853, Nightingale took over a squalid hospital in London and ran it cleanly and efficiently.

In 1854, Nightingale was asked to help the British army doctors in the Crimean War. Her work in one of the military hospitals there soon made her world famous.

For the rest of her life, Nightingale worked to reform hospitals and nursing practices.

Florence Nightingale died in 1910, aged 90.

BEFORE: Wounded British soldiers huddle in appalling conditions at the hospital in Scutari, Turkey.

IN THE EARLY 1800s, hospitals were squalid pits of disease, where patients were as likely to die as to be cured. Yet the work of one woman brought about a dramatic change. *The History News* pays tribute to Florence Nightingale.

IMAGINE THIS. The year is 1854. You're a British soldier sent to fight the Russians in Crimea, a region near Turkey.

You've been seriously wounded and taken to the British army hospital in Scutari, Turkey. Sick soldiers sprawl on the floor, wrapped only in blankets caked with filth. There are no beds, no tables or chairs, not even cups for bringing you water. There's also the terrible stink of sewage.

The few attendants cannot cope with all the sick soldiers. You're lucky if they manage to feed you once a day.

This was the scene that confronted William Russell, a journalist from *The Times* newspaper of London, when he visited Scutari in October 1854.

His reports caused outrage back in Britain. The government was so embarrassed that they decided someone had to try to improve matters.

And one name kept cropping up — Florence Nightingale.

NIGHTINGALE TO THE RESCUE!

For years, Nightingale had been thinking about ways to improve hospital care and conditions.

The government was familiar with her work and decided to hire her to go to Scutari with a team of 38 nurses.

At first, the army was furious that a woman had come to help them. But the situation was so desperate that they soon let her get to work.

Nightingale was one of the first people to understand clearly the importance of hygiene in preventing disease. She had the wards scrubbed from top to bottom, and the patients washed. She also arranged for the government back home to send over medicine and bandages.

Before Nightingale had arrived, 20 out of every 50 soldiers admitted to the hospital had died.

MESS!

AN UPHILL STRUGGLE

Illustrated by LUIGI GALANTE

By the war's end, only one in 50 failed to survive.

And by the time she returned home to Britain, Nightingale's nighttime visits to sick soldiers had made her famous as "the lady with the lamp."

She was a national heroine, and the public donated nearly $70,000 for her to continue her work.

There was much to be done. Civilian hospitals were almost as dirty as military ones, and the untrained nurses had a reputation for being lazy, careless, and often drunk.

But Nightingale soon changed all that. She hounded politicians to make improvements and wrote books on the best way to organize hospitals.

She also used all the money she'd been given to set up the The Nightingale School for Nurses in London. Soon, all nurses were highly qualified.

By her death in 1910, Florence Nightingale had created a revolution in hospital care. At last, nurses and patients were treated with respect, and the foul, filthy conditions of Scutari had long faded into history. ✚

WOMEN CAN'T BE DOCTORS! That was the view of most people in the 1800s. It took a young American, Elizabeth Blackwell, to prove them wrong — as she told the *The History News* in 1849.

PEOPLE HAVE laughed at me and called me crazy. I've been shouted at in the street and I've even been told that I'm a disgrace to women. But I'm still determined to practice as a doctor.

All I want to do is to live my life in the best possible way. And four years ago, I decided I could do nothing more useful than become a doctor. No woman had ever been one before, it's true — but it was time for that to change!

First, I spent two years working as a teacher in order to raise money for my studies. At the same time, I read medical books and learned about the basics of anatomy. I felt that I was well prepared.

But when I applied to join medical schools, I was rejected — simply because I was female! One doctor even had the nerve to suggest I should dress up as a man to attend lectures.

That was not what I wanted. I would qualify as a woman — or not at all. Finally, the University of Geneva, in New York, voted to let me join its program.

This was my chance at last — and I jumped at it! I studied hard and have just graduated at the top of the class.

But my struggle is far from over. I am a working doctor now, but I still face a lot of prejudice. It's worth it, though. My story stands as an example to the world — women can be doctors too! ✚

AFTER: Nightingale surveys the clean wards.

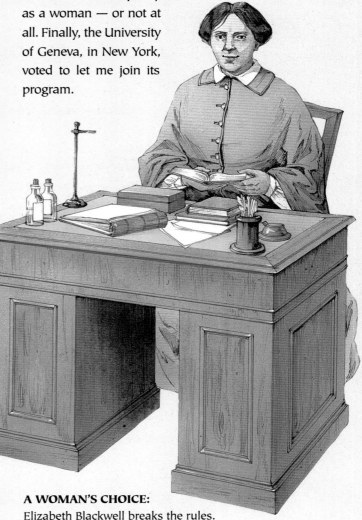

A WOMAN'S CHOICE:
Elizabeth Blackwell breaks the rules.

AHEAD OF HIS TIME

OUR HIDDEN

Illustrated by GINO D'ACHILLE

TWO HUNDRED years before Louis Pasteur, the world of miniature life forms was discovered by Antoni van Leeuwenhoek. *The History News* looks at his career.

LEEUWENHOEK was no scientist — he was a cloth merchant from Delft, in Holland — yet in 1674 he made a remarkable scientific find. He was the first person ever to see the tiny creatures we now call bacteria.

It all began when Leeuwenhoek started making microscopes to study the quality of different fabrics.

MICROSCOPE MAN: Antoni van Leeuwenhoek.

He began to record anything he saw and soon discovered an amazing thing. Almost everywhere he looked he found microscopic organisms, all smaller than the tip of a pin. They lived in drops of rain, in pond water, and even in the saliva from Leeuwenhoek's mouth.

But Leeuwenhoek didn't recognize the most important thing about the bacteria he saw — that some of them caused disease. For that, the world had to wait for Pasteur. ‡

STRANGE NEW WORLD: Leeuwenhoek's sketches of some of the weird organisms he studied.

ALL AROUND us lurk invisible life forms — and some of them are killers! In 1861, the French scientist Louis Pasteur told *The History News* how he made the vital link between tiny organisms and disease.

❓ What exactly was your great discovery?
Well, before I started my research in 1858, disease wasn't properly understood.

Scientists knew that minute living things, which we now call bacteria, were present in diseased parts of the body — we saw them under our microscopes. But we didn't know that some of them actually *caused* illness.

We thought that they must be produced as diseased parts of the body started to decay. This idea was called the theory of spontaneous generation, in which rotting flesh made new life forms.

BAD WINE GIVES CLUES

But after I began my experiments, I realized that we'd gotten the story backward. The bacteria came from outside the body, and by attacking it in vast numbers, they caused it to decay.

❓ How did you find that out?
I wasn't thinking about medicine at the time. I was studying wine to learn why it went bad.

With my microscope I could see millions of bacteria living in the bad wine. However, if I heated the wine up, the bacteria were killed.

I also found that this same wine stayed free of bacteria as long as it was kept in a sealed container. But once I took the lid off, living bacteria reappeared and the wine went bad.

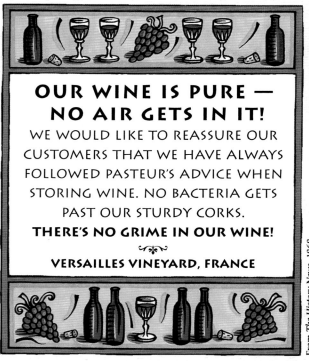
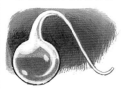

ENEMIES DISCOVERED

I guessed that the bacteria made the wine bad and that they came from the air itself! If they'd been made by the wine, they'd have come back while the lid was still on, wouldn't they have?

❓ Were other scientists excited by all this?

Not at first! I had to try several experiments in order to prove to them that airborne bacteria made things go bad.

First of all, I sucked air through a cotton cloth to collect bacteria. Then I put the cloth in some broth that had been boiled until it was pure. The broth was then sealed — but it still went bad. And the bacteria that caused this could have come only from the air sucked through the cloth.

As final proof, I had some special glass flasks made with long narrow necks that were bent into an "S" shape, like swans' necks. I put pure broth inside and left them.

EYE SPY: Using a powerful microscope, Pasteur tracks down dangerous bacteria.

The flasks were not sealed, but the broth stayed pure because even airborne particles as minute as bacteria couldn't get past the tightly twisted S-bends. However, when I snapped the necks off the flasks, the bacteria reached the broth and it went bad very quickly.

❓ But what's this got to do with disease?

A great deal! Just as some airborne bacteria can make broth go bad, other sorts can cause serious diseases.

When these bacteria land on warm, moist parts of the body, they start to multiply. A few bacteria can turn into millions in an hour or so, and their unlucky victim soon becomes ill.

My work means that we finally know who our hidden enemies are. But this is just the beginning of the fight. Now we must look for ways to protect ourselves against their deadly menace! ✚

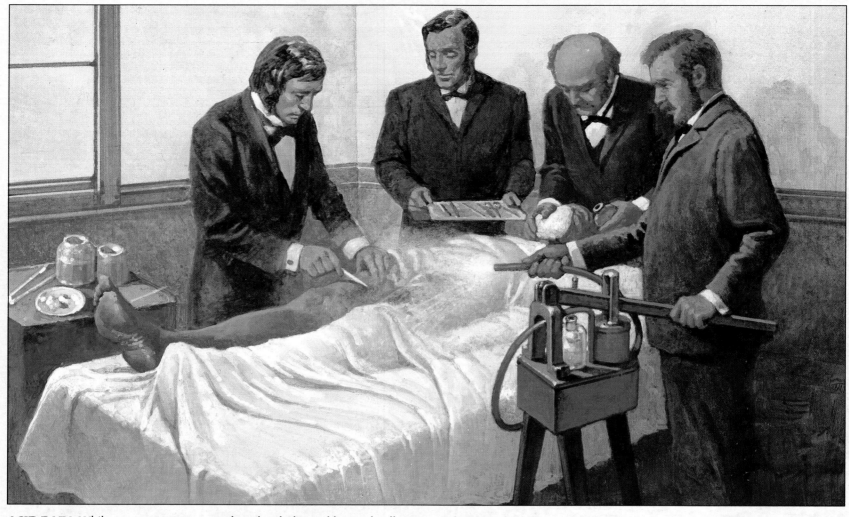

ACID RAIN: While a surgeon operates, a fog of carbolic acid keeps deadly germs at bay.

LISTER'S LIFESAVER

Illustrated by GINO D'ACHILLE

IMAGINE AN operating room filled with a fine mist of acid that stings everything it touches. It may sound crazy, yet this acid was the greatest lifesaver in surgical history. In 1869, *The History News* reported on British surgeon Joseph Lister's momentous invention.

IN THE PAST, patients facing a major operation knew they risked death — not from the surgeon's knife, but from an infected wound. If germs got into the wound and turned it septic, little could be done about it. The area would begin to rot, the decay would spread, and the patient would die.

But now everything has changed, thanks to Professor Joseph Lister of Glasgow University.

It was reading about the work of Louis Pasteur that made Lister realize fatal infections are caused by bacteria. He became determined to kill these germs before they killed any more of his patients.

In 1865, Lister had an inspiration. He decided to wash his instruments and his patients' wounds in carbolic acid, which was sometimes used to clean sewers.

And the experiment worked! Lister discovered that carbolic acid is an antiseptic — destroying bacteria before they can infect wounds.

SALVATION SPRAY

Inspired by this success, Lister tried to reduce the risk of infection further. He invented a spraying machine that could fill a whole operating room with a fine fog of acid during an operation.

In the four years since then, Lister's results have been sensational. Before the spray, almost half the patients he operated on died from infection. Now, remarkably, just fifteen out of every hundred die!

Today, other surgeons are starting to use Lister's invention, and their death rates are also falling. Together with the new standards of hospital hygiene being introduced by Florence Nightingale, Lister's spray is going to revolutionize medicine.

There are drawbacks to his methods, though, as *The History News*'s reporter discovered when he talked to one unhappy surgeon, who preferred to remain anonymous.

"I can't argue with Lister's results," he said, "but it's his spraying machine that's the real nightmare. How would you like to spend your days operating in a room filled with carbolic acid vapor? It makes your eyes sting, cracks open your skin, and rots your clothes.

And some unlucky assistant has to stand there for several hours pumping the stuff from the machine. He can't stop for a moment in case germs get through, so by the end of the day, he's dead on his feet!"

But even this doctor admits that the spray *has* revolutionized surgery.

"A boy came in last week with a badly gashed and broken leg. In the old days, the safest option was to cut it off. But nowadays I don't have to worry about infection. So I just flooded the wound with carbolic acid and reset the bones. The boy will walk again."

SAFER SURGERY

Throughout Europe and America there have been countless similar cases. Joseph Lister's acid spray has won a decisive victory in the long war against infection — surely a few stinging eyes is a price well worth paying! ✚

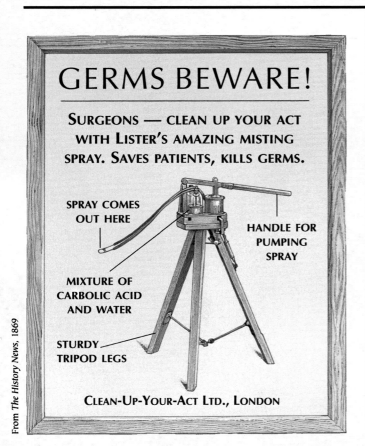

ONE MORE SAFE STEP

Illustrated by MAXINE HAMIL

LISTER'S ANTISEPTIC spray made surgery safer for the patient, but less comfortable for the surgeon. A better method was soon developed by two German doctors and is still in use today. They described their ideas in this letter to *The History News* in 1886.

Dear Editor,

We think we should tell the world about our breakthrough in surgical hygiene.

For several years now we have been working on a new alternative to Lister's antiseptic system. It is just as safe as his spray, but it doesn't sting at all!

Lister's antiseptics kill the deadly germs that get into the operating room. But our system goes one better. It keeps germs out of the operating room altogether! We have named it the aseptic method.

Under this system, everything is cleaned before it is taken into the operating room — and not simply the surgical instruments, but also the clothes, and even the air that comes into the room.

High temperatures kill bacteria just as well as carbolic acid does. So hats, aprons and rubber boots are blasted by hot steam to sterilize them all before they are worn. Instruments are first boiled, then stored in containers filled with carbolic acid.

The air is heated to sterilize it, before it is forced through incredibly fine cotton filters. Only after all this is the air pumped into specially built operating rooms.

There is no need for choking clouds of acid! Our methods have shut out germs from surgery forever!

Yours faithfully,

Professor Ernst von Bergmann and Professor Gustav Neuber

Germany, November 11, 1886

X RAYS SHOW BONES!

Illustrated by LAWRIE TAYLOR

IN 1895, the discovery of X rays led to a revolution in medical practice. It was now possible to see through the skin to the bones hidden beneath! But the public was worried by the rays, as these letters sent to *The History News* reveal.

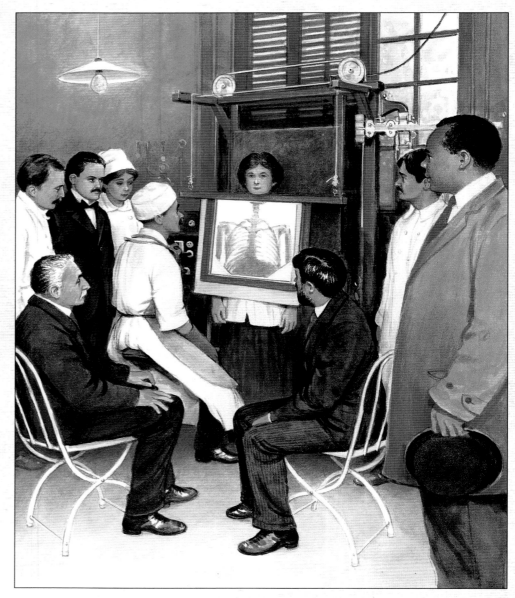

INTERNAL AFFAIRS: A fluoroscope allows doctors to watch the human body at work.

Yesterday, my dear daughter, Louisa, broke her arm in a fall. Our doctor wishes to x-ray her, but I am worried about this strange new invention. Why does he need to do this?
Yours faithfully,
Mrs. Anne Ziety

Madam, please put your mind at rest. Your doctor is simply following the most up-to-date methods and using an X ray to look at how Louisa's bones are broken. This will help him figure out how to mend them.

Louisa will be asked to stand between an X-ray machine and a special photographic plate. Rays from the X-ray machine will go through her skin and muscles and turn the plate dark.

However, rays cannot pass through bone, so the shapes of Louisa's bones — and any breaks in them — will show up as light areas on the photographic plate.

This vital information will help your doctor heal Louisa's arm perfectly.

Everyone's talking about X rays, but who discovered them?
Sincerely,
Lady Knowsy

They were discovered by Wilhelm Roentgen, a German scientist working at Würzberg University. He announced the find on December 28, 1895, and caused a sensation. In only a few weeks, scientists throughout the world were busy building machines to see inside the human body.

I would like to buy an X-ray machine for my hospital. Is it worth the expense?
Yours, Dr. Lancelot Boyle

You can't do without one! An X-ray machine is vital for studying bones and even large organs, like the heart. And it makes it easy to find hard objects, such as bullets, so you can quickly remove them.

But you should also think about buying a fluoroscope. This X-ray machine doesn't take single pictures. Instead, it casts moving shadows of the bones and organs onto a screen, allowing doctors to see the insides of the body in action.

My doctor insists he needs to x-ray me. Is he just trying to see me without my clothes on?
Yours faithfully,
Miss Seamore-Legg

Have no fear, X rays are perfectly respectable!

They pass through flesh as easily as they do through clothes, and all your doctor will see will be your bones.

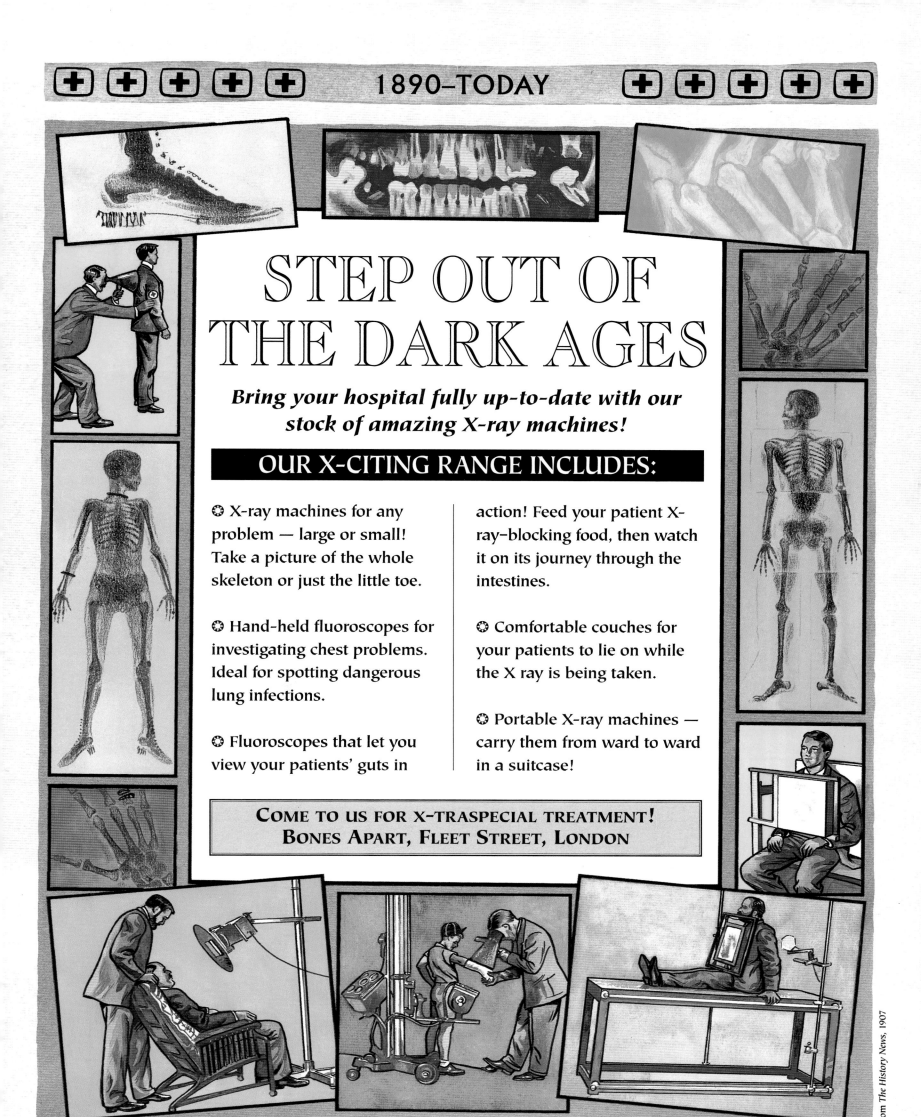

IT'S MOLD MAGIC

Illustrated by LAWRIE TAYLOR

FABULOUS FUNGUS: Alexander Fleming with his miraculous discovery.

IT'S HARD TO IMAGINE anything less exciting than a moldy dish. Yet it was this that put Scottish doctor Alexander Fleming on the track of one of the world's most powerful medicines. In 1942, Fleming told *The History News* the story of penicillin.

IT ALL BEGAN about 14 years ago at St. Mary's Hospital in London. I've never been very tidy, and my laboratory was piled high with glass dishes containing old samples of bacteria.

For many years I had been hunting for a new kind of medicine — one that could be swallowed to kill dangerous bacteria inside the body. But after years of work, I'd yet to make a breakthrough.

Well, the dirty dishes were in the sink, ready to be washed. I was about to disinfect them when I saw a bluish gray mold, growing on one of them.

Then I looked closer and noticed something peculiar. The bacteria all around the edges of the mold had died. When I saw that, I forgot all about doing the dishes!

MOLDY MYSTERY

Could it really have been the mold that killed the germs? I quickly took a sample of the mold and tested it. With growing astonishment, I found it contained a chemical that killed many kinds of bacteria — including the ones that caused deadly diseases, like scarlet fever, diphtheria, and pneumonia.

The mold is actually very widespread — you've probably seen it growing on rotten fruit! Its name is *Penicillium notatum,* so I called this remarkable chemical "penicillin."

However, the mold juice itself produced only very small quantities of penicillin — not enough to be effective inside the body. And to make enough for medicine would be a difficult task.

I had other pressing work at the time, and I was forced to leave the development of penicillin to others. So it wasn't until 1938 that Howard Florey and Ernst Chain — two brilliant scientists at Oxford — got working on penicillin.

INCREDIBLE CURE

After two years, enough pure penicillin had been extracted from the mold for it to be tested on some diseased mice. The results were amazing. Mice given a dose of the drug were fine and well a few hours later, while those without it died.

Then came the final test. Penicillin was given to human patients — to dying people who had no other hope left. And it cured them!

In the future, penicillin will save millions. Not bad going for something that began with a single dirty dish! ✚

HOPE FOR THE DYING: An American doctor treats a wounded soldier with a penicillin injection.

ESCAPE FROM DEATH

Illustrated by STEVE NOON

TO DOCTORS treating casualties during the horrors of World War II, penicillin was the "wonder drug." In 1944, *The History News* sent a reporter to the battlefront in France to find out why.

SOLDIERS wounded in the terrible battles now raging in northern Europe have been dying in the thousands from severe blood poisoning.

But at last there is new hope. Laboratories in America are working hard around the clock to produce vast amounts of penicillin — the amazing new drug that fights bacterial infection deep inside the bloodstream.

Yesterday I followed a shipment of penicillin powder to a field hospital in northern France to see the results of this mighty effort.

As our jeep screeched to a halt, several nurses ran over and rushed the lifesaving medicine into tents, where the wounded soldiers were waiting.

In one tent was a pilot whose plane had crashed in flames. His burns had quickly become infected, blood poisoning had set in, and he was gripped by a raging fever.

Death was just hours away — unless penicillin could save him. A doctor took the yellow powder and carefully dissolved it in a mixture of salt and water, which was fed by tubes into the pilot's arm. Slowly, the vital liquid began to drip into his veins. Now all we could do was wait and hope.

After only 30 minutes the pilot's temperature had fallen by more than two degrees. His pulse had slowed, and the color was gradually returning to his ashen face.

BROUGHT BACK TO LIFE

In only two hours, the pilot's temperature was normal again. The doctor nodded with satisfaction. "He'll survive," he said.

And sure enough, just seven hours after getting the first dose, the pilot was sitting up and asking for a cup of coffee. The amazing transformation was complete.

Scenes like this send out a clear, triumphant message to all those people making penicillin in far-off America.

Keep the effort going! Every dose of penicillin you make may save a soldier's life! ✚

BLOOD SWAPPING

FOR CENTURIES, doctors tried saving patients' lives by giving them a new supply of blood. But blood transfusion has always been a risky business. . . .

✪ **1667:** Jean Denys, a French doctor, carries out the first transfer of blood, from a lamb to a boy. The boy survives, but many other early experiments that use animal blood are fatal.

✪ **1829:** James Blundell, an English physician, is the first doctor to save a patient's life by transferring blood from one patient to another.

✪ **1901:** An Austrian physician named Karl Landsteiner makes the crucial discovery that there are different types of human blood.

Up until now, many blood transfusions fail because the donor and the patient have different blood types. When that happens, the two bloods can't mix properly and the patient quickly dies.

By giving patients the same type of blood as their own, they are more likely to survive the transfusion.

✪ **1914:** A chemical is developed that keeps stored blood from solidifying. Now blood can be given to patients whenever and wherever they need it! ✠

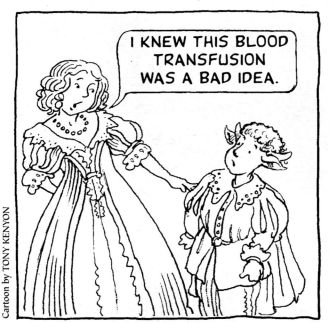

I KNEW THIS BLOOD TRANSFUSION WAS A BAD IDEA.

Cartoon by TONY KENYON

A CHANGE

Illustrated by CHRISTIAN HOOK

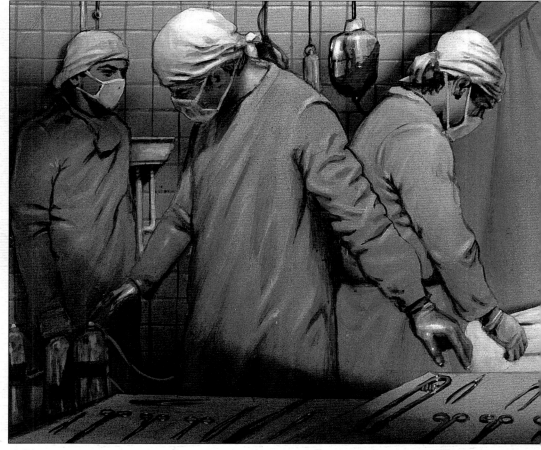

HEART TO HEART: Dr. Christiaan Barnard prepares to remove his patient's diseased heart.

USING THE DEAD to treat the sick sounds sinister, but it has proved to be a great lifesaver. On December 4, 1967, *The History News* broke the story of the world's first heart transplant operation.

YESTERDAY, the Groote Schuur Hospital in Cape Town, South Africa, was mobbed by reporters. They didn't want to miss the most exciting medical event of the decade.

Louis Washkansky, a 55-year-old man dying from heart disease, had been given the heart of a 25-year-old woman who'd been killed in a car crash.

Dr. Christiaan Barnard, the surgeon who led the transplant team, held a packed press conference to give details of the extraordinary operation.

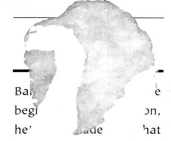

Ba... ...e begi... ...on, he'... ...de ...hat

a transplant was the patient's only hope of survival. Barnard also had to be certain that the dead woman's blood type was similar to Washkansky's, so that it would be easier for his body to accept the new heart as his own.

As soon as the donor had been declared dead, half of the transplant team opened her chest and removed her heart.

Meanwhile, the other doctors carefully removed Washkansky's damaged heart. A pump attached to the blood vessels in

OF HEART!

MOVING PARTS

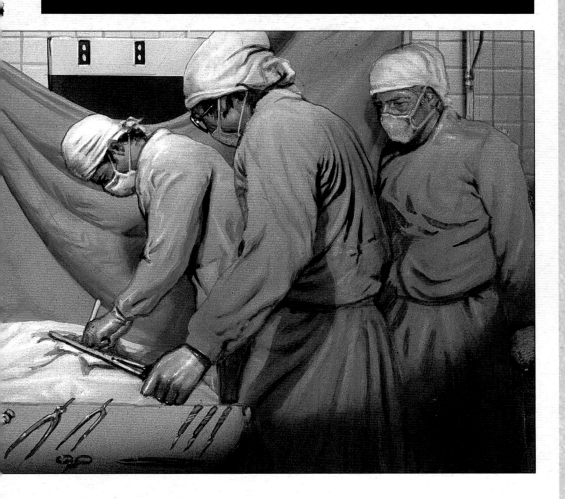

IF YOUR BODY is wearing out and parts of it are failing, what can you do? Just turn to *The History News*'s guide to body replacements.

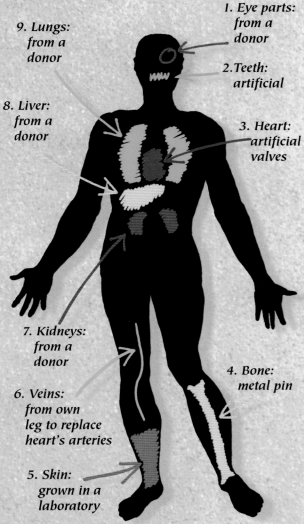

9. Lungs: from a donor

1. Eye parts: from a donor

2. Teeth: artificial

8. Liver: from a donor

3. Heart: artificial valves

7. Kidneys: from a donor

4. Bone: metal pin

6. Veins: from own leg to replace heart's arteries

5. Skin: grown in a laboratory

one leg took over for the heart and kept the man's blood circulating.

Now came the most dramatic stage of all — the transplant itself. The new heart was placed into Washkansky's chest. Then Barnard connected it to all the surrounding blood vessels by sewing them with a double layer of strong silk stitches.

When he had finished came the moment of truth. Had the four-hour

operation worked? The entire team held their breath as electric shocks were used to try to restart the new heart.

Success! At the first shock the heart began beating. Then the pump that had been circulating Washkansky's blood was removed, and his new heart took over.

Barnard is optimistic that ᵏᵛ will su   he v   is   nt   ew hope   ɡ of heart disease ✚

EDITOR'S NOTE: Sadly, Washkansky died 17 days later. The drugs that were helping his body accept the new heart stopped him from fighting off a fatal lung infection.

But this was the start of a new age. Many transplants, of hearts and other vital organs, have taken place since then, and a great many of them have been extremely successful.

REPLACEMENT parts can come from many sources. These days, artificially made parts are commonly used to help diseased organs last longer.

Some parts can be supplied by donors, while others, such as skin, can be grown in a laboratory.

Most amazing of all, animals will soon be specially bred so that their organs can be transplanted into humans' bodies. ✚

WHAT NOW?

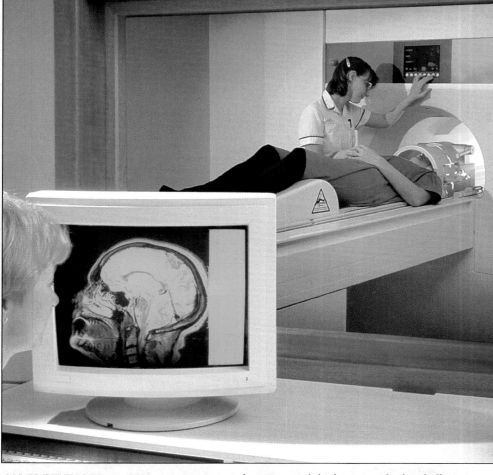

ALL IS REVEALED: An MRI scanner gives a clear image of the brain inside the skull.

THROUGHOUT this book we've looked at the greatest medical developments of the past. But what about today's big breakthroughs? What new inventions are taking modern doctors by storm? *The History News* asked three experts.

THE SURGEON

"The most significant change I've experienced is endoscopic surgery, which was developed in the 1980s. When I first saw it, I could hardly believe my eyes, but now it's quite a common procedure.

In the past, I had to make large cuts into a patient's body in order to reach the diseased area.

With endoscopic surgery I merely have to make a small hole and insert a thin flexible telescope through it. Using this, I can see deep inside the body. Then, with tiny surgical tools inserted through another small opening, I can carry out any necessary surgery.

Because the holes are very small, they cause much less pain to the patient than a gaping wound. They heal far more quickly, too.

Endoscopic surgery has brought medicine into a new age."

THE DOCTOR

"My job as a hospital doctor has been made much easier by the amazing new machines now used in hospitals.

In the past, the brain and many other areas of the body were impossible to see, even with X rays. But these new machines can help me locate the source of any problem.

For example, there's the Magnetic Resonance Imaging (MRI) scanner, which was invented in the 1970s. This machine produces astonishingly accurate pictures of the inside of the body — not just the bones, as X rays do, but organs as well.

Now that I can see exactly what is wrong, I can treat my patients far more effectively."

THE RESEARCHER

"Gene therapy is the most exciting advance happening in medical research today.

Every cell in your body contains genes — the chemical instructions that tell cells how to work properly. Some of the most dangerous diseases — such as cystic fibrosis, which harms people's lungs — happen because sufferers are born with damaged genes.

We researchers have been studying genes since the 1950s, though it took us until 1990 to understand them well enough to treat damaged ones directly. Soon we will be able to substitute unhealthy genes with healthier replacements made in the laboratory.

Our research should make it possible for us to prevent a vast number of diseases from occurring in the first place. What an incredible leap forward for medicine!"

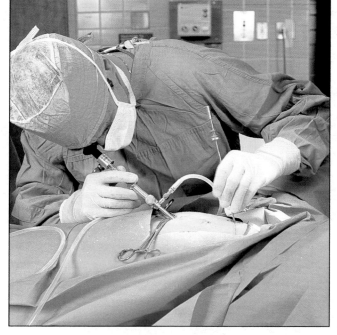

THE KINDEST CUT: Endoscopic surgery causes little pain.

TIME LINE

✴ 8000 B.C.
Prehistoric people perform trepanning operations.

✴ 2700 B.C.
Imhotep, the first doctor whose name is written down in history, treats patients in ancient Egypt.

✴ About 2500 B.C.
Acupuncture is developed in ancient China.

✴ About 600 B.C.
Susruta pioneers many new surgical techniques in ancient India.

✴ 460 B.C.
Hippocrates is born in ancient Greece.

✴ A.D. 14–117
The Roman Empire grows to its greatest extent.

✴ A.D. 160–200
Galen writes the books that will form the basis of European medicine for the next 1,400 years.

✴ A.D. 300–476
The vast Roman Empire collapses.

✴ A.D. 400–1500
Muslim civilizations in the Middle East keep medical learning alive. Meanwhile, Europe enters an age of ignorance.

✴ From 1100
Medical writings from ancient Greece and Rome are translated back from Muslim Arabic into Latin.

✴ 1330–51
The Black Death spreads across Asia and Europe.

✴ Early 1500s
In Italy, the Renaissance is at its height, leading to new interest in medicine and the human body.

✴ 1518
The Spanish take smallpox to Mexico. Half the population is killed.

✴ 1537–52
Ambroise Paré develops improved treatments for battle wounds.

✴ 1540–43
Andreas Vesalius dissects human bodies, disproving many of Galen's ideas.

✴ About 1590
Microscope invented by Dutchman Hans Janssen.

✴ About 1593
Thermometer invented by Galileo in Italy.

✴ 1628
William Harvey shows that the heart pumps blood around the body.

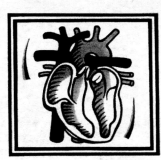

✴ 1674
Antoni van Leeuwenhoek describes bacteria for the first time.

✴ 1717
Lady Montagu brings the news of smallpox variolation to Britain.

✴ 1796
Edward Jenner vaccinates a boy against smallpox.

✴ 1818
Stethoscope invented by French physician René Laënnec.

✴ 1846
William Morton first uses ether as an anesthetic.

✴ 1849
Elizabeth Blackwell is the first woman doctor in America.

✴ 1854
Florence Nightingale goes to the Crimea and cleans up the military hospital.

✴ 1860
The Nightingale School for Nurses is opened in London.

NIGHTINGALE

✴ 1861
Louis Pasteur proves that bacteria carried in the air cause things to go bad.

✴ 1865
Joseph Lister first tries out carbolic acid as an antiseptic.

✴ 1886
Ernst von Bergmann and Gustav Neuber develop aseptic methods.

✴ 1895
X rays are discovered by Wilhelm Roentgen.

✴ 1901
Karl Landsteiner is the first to discover there are different types of blood.

✴ 1928
Penicillin is discovered by Alexander Fleming.

✴ 1938–41
Howard Florey and Ernst Chain develop penicillin as a medicine.

✴ 1967
Dr. Christiaan Barnard performs the first human heart transplant.

✴ 1976
MRI scanner first used on the human body.

✴ 1979
A worldwide campaign of vaccination wipes out smallpox forever.

✴ 1980s
Endoscopic surgery is first developed.

✴ 1990
Doctors first use gene replacement as a treatment.

INDEX

A
Abbott, Gilbert 16, 17
acupuncture 4
anatomy 10, 11, 19
anesthetics 16–17
antiseptics 22–23
apothecaries 13
aseptic method 23

B
bacteria 9, 20, 21, 22, 23, 26, 27
 discovery of 20–21
barbers 13
Barnard, Dr. Christiaan 28–29
Bergmann, Ernst von 23
Black Death 9
Blackwell, Elizabeth 19
blood circulation 12, 29
blood transfusions 28
blood types 28
Blundell, James 28

C
carbolic acid,
 see antiseptics
Chain, Ernst 26
Chinese medicine 4, 15
chloroform 17
corpses, medical uses of 10, 28–29
cowpox 14, 15
Crimean War 18

D
Denys, Jean 28
doctors, in 1600s 13
 women 19

E
endoscopic surgery 30
ether 16–17

F
false body parts 5, 7, 11, 29
Fleming, Alexander 26
Florey, Howard 26

G
Galen, Claudius 7, 8, 10, 12
gene therapy 30
germs, see bacteria

H, I
Harvey, William 12
heart, study of 12
 transplant of 28–29
Hippocrates 6, 7, 8
hospitals 7, 18–19, 22, 23, 24, 25, 27, 28
Hunter, John 14
hygiene 6–7, 18–19, 22–23

Indian medicine,
 ancient 4, 5, 7

J, K
Jenner, Edward 14–15
Ko Hung 15

L
Landsteiner, Karl 28
Leeuwenhoek, Antoni van 20
Lister, Joseph 22–23

M
medieval cures 8
microscopes 20, 21
midwives 13
Montagu, Lady Mary Wortley 14, 15
Morton, William 16–17
MRI scanners 30

N
Neuber, Gustav 23
Nightingale, Florence 18–19, 22
nitrous oxide 17
nursing reform,
 see Nightingale

O
operations 3, 5, 11, 13, 16–17, 22–23, 28–29, 30
organ transplants 28–29

P
Paré, Ambroise 11
Pasteur, Louis 20–21, 22
penicillin 26, 27
Phipps, James 15
physicians 13, 28
plague, see Black Death
prehistoric medicine 3

R
Renaissance 10
Roentgen, Wilhelm 24
Rome, ancient 6–7, 8, 12

S
smallpox 14–15
stethoscopes 2
superstition 3, 8
surgeons 4, 13
 see also operations
surgery, see operations
Susruta 5

T, V
trepanning 3

vaccination 14–15
variation 14, 15
Vesalius, Andreas 10

W
Washkansky, Louis 28, 29
Wells, Horace 17
World Health Organization 15

X
X rays 24, 25

Some dates in this book have the letters "B.C." after them. B.C. stands for "Before Christ" — so 300 B.C. means 300 years before the birth of Christ. "A.D." means after the birth of Christ.

Please visit our web site at: www.garethstevens.com
For a free color catalog describing Gareth Stevens' list of high-quality books and multimedia programs, call 1-800-542-2595 (USA) or 1-800-461-9120 (Canada). Gareth Stevens Publishing's Fax: (414) 332-3567.

Gareth Stevens Publishing thanks Dr. Norman Engbring of the Medical College of Wisconsin, Milwaukee, Wisconsin, for his professional help with the information in this book.

Library of Congress Cataloging-in-Publication Data

Gates, Phil.
 Medicine / by Phil Gates.
  p. cm. -- (History news)
 Includes bibliographical references and index.
 ISBN 0-8368-2877-1 (lib. bdg.)
 1. Medicine--History--Juvenile literature. [1. Medicine--History.]
 I. Title. II. History news (Milwaukee, Wis.)
 R133.5.G37 2001
 610:9--dc21   2001025021

This edition published in 2001 by
Gareth Stevens Publishing
A World Almanac Education Group Company
330 West Olive Street, Suite 100
Milwaukee, Wisconsin 53212 USA

Text © 1997 by Philip Gates. Illustrations © 1997 by Walker Books Ltd. First U.S. edition published by Candlewick Press, 2067 Massachusetts Ave., Cambridge, MA 02140.

The History News: Medicine
Author: Phil Gates
Consultant: Dr. Ghislaine Lawrence, Curator of Clinical Medicine, The Science Museum, London, U.K.
Editors: Lesley Ann Daniels and Jonathan Stroud
Designer: Louise Jackson
Gareth Stevens Editor: Monica Rausch
Gareth Stevens Designer: Scott Krall

Advertisement illustrations by: Pip Adams 8b; Vanessa Card 4tr; Sandra Doyle 4br; Maxine Hamil 2tl, 2br, 6br, 12bl, 20bm; Micheala Stewart 7bl; Pete Visscher 2tr, 2m, 7bm, 23b; Peter Ware 25; Mike White 11ml, 11tl, 11bl, 17bl, 20br, 26br.

Decorative borders and small illustrations by: Peter Bull 3br; Caroline Church 15m, 21b; Jonathan Hair 29r; Maxine Hamil 1, 7r, 17r, 18l, 23r, 27br; Emily Hare 4tl, 5b; Mike White 15, 20tl, 20bl.

Photograph: The Science Photo Library, p. 30.

With thanks to: Linden Artists; Temple Rogers; The Garden Studio; Virgil Pomfret Agency; The Science Photo Library, London; The Imperial War Museum, London; Florence Nightingale Museum, London; Alexander Fleming Laboratory Museum, London; Groote Schuur Hospital Transplant Museum, Cape Town

SOURCES
Christiaan Barnard, *A Human Cardiac Transplant*
Sir H. W. Florey, *Penicillin: A Survey*
Galen, *On Anatomy*
William Harvey, *The Movement of the Heart*
Hippocrates, *The Hippocratic Collection*
Edward Jenner, *An Enquiry into the Causes and Effects of Variola Vaccinae*
Antoni van Leeuwenhoek, *The Secrets of Nature Discovered*
Florence Nightingale, *Notes on Nursing*
Ambroise Paré, *Surgery*
Louis Pasteur, *Memoirs on Organic Corpuscles . . .*
Wilhelm Roentgen, *On a New Kind of Ray*
Susruta, *Susruta Samhita*
Andreas Vesalius, *Fabric of the Human Body*